WHEN THE RAILS RAN WEST

in 1866, the greatest railroading achievement in the United States had started. Here is the dramatic story of three years of exciting adventure as the railroad's iron tracks reach further West each day on the long route to California.

New towns spring up on the Great Plains, railroad work-gangs race against blizzards and time, and hostile Indians challenge the white man's hated "fire road." The great moment arrives when Union Pacific and Central Pacific tracks are joined by a golden spike at Promontory Summit, Utah.

From old diaries and newspaper stories of the day, this era comes vividly to life. Prints, paintings, and photographs of the period enrich this authentic account of a time when a new kind of pioneering adventure opened for all Americans.

This book is one of the How They Lived series, developed by Garrard to give meaning to the study of American history. Young people will find a deeper understanding and more lasting appreciation of history and geography as they see life in the past through the eyes of those who lived it.

When the Rails Ran West

CALAVERAS COUNTY
SCHOOLS LIBRARY
SAN ANDREAS, CALIFORNIA

When the Rails Ran West

BY JAMES McCAGUE

ILLUSTRATED BY VICTOR MAYS

GARRARD PUBLISHING COMPANY
CHAMPAIGN, ILLINOIS

Picture credits:

Contents

1. The Fire Road

One August morning in 1866 the Sioux chief, Spotted Tail, led his band of eighteen mounted warriors across the shallow Platte River. He was hunting the strange new "fire road" which had come to the Nebraska plains.

"Fire road" was the Indians' name for the white men's railroad. They called it that because of the big, smoking steam engines. No railroad had ever been seen on these western

WYOMING

SOUTH DAKOTA

Missouri River

IOWA

NEBRASKA

North Platte River

Cheyenne

Laramie

Plum Creek

Omaha

Julesburg

Platte River

COLORADO

UNION PACIFIC RAILROAD

CENTRAL PACIFIC RAILROAD

plains before. The Sioux were not happy to see one now, either. They knew the trains would bring more white men to kill the buffaloes and spoil the Indians' hunting grounds.

Spotted Tail always had been friendly toward white men. But he did not feel friendly now.

Soon the warriors saw an amazing sight. There, at the end of a shiny iron track, stood a string of wooden cars. Some were so big they looked like houses on wheels.

Engines with tall diamond-shaped smoke-stacks hissed and panted. Piles of iron rails

Friendly Indians watch as work crews lay rails that
will bring the strange "fire road" westward.

and kegs and boxes stood by the track. Nearly
five hundred workmen bustled to and fro. The
clang of hammers on spikes filled the air.

As the Indians drew near, many workmen
dropped their tools and seized their rifles. But
Spotted Tail lifted his arm and made the peace
sign. One of his braves could speak a little
English. Spotted Tail told him to say that the
Sioux just wanted to see what the white men
were doing.

The leader of the workmen told them they
were welcome.

8

The braves got down from their ponies. For a while they watched the men at work. But they could not understand so much hustle and bustle. Then they were shown through the work train.

Four cars in the train were bigger than the rest. One of these was a mess hall, with long tables and benches. Another was half mess hall too. The rest of it held a kitchen and an office for the leader, or track boss.

Next came two bunk cars. Three rows of bunks, one above another, were built along both sides of each car. An aisle ran down the middle. On the ceiling were racks with hundreds of rifles. The white men made sure the Sioux saw the rifles, which were there in case unfriendly Indians attacked the train.

Other cars were full of sacks of flour, potatoes, and other food. In one, butchers were cutting up sides of beef for cooking. Another car was a bakery, with men just taking hot, crusty loaves of bread from the ovens. In still another, a burly blacksmith worked at his blazing forge, mending tools.

A herd of cattle grazed nearby. They were driven right along with the train to supply fresh meat.

The Indians looked at all these things and
said nothing. They could see that these "fire
road" men were very strong.

But the Sioux could show off too. They told
a workman to stick his shovel upright in the
dirt. Then, whipping out their bows and arrows,
they all shot at it. A young railroad man
named E. C. Lockwood wrote about all this
afterward. He said that every arrow except
one whistled straight through the hole in the
shovel's handle, from about sixty feet away.

The white men watched with sidelong glances
as they worked. They couldn't help thinking
that they would make bigger targets for Indian
arrows than that shovel.

When the Sioux had put aside their bows, the foreman invited Spotted Tail for a ride on one of the engines. The chief was not very eager to go. To him the locomotive seemed like a fire-breathing monster. But he climbed aboard. A Sioux was too proud to show fear.

As the engine chugged down the track the other braves leaped on their ponies to race with it. Soon they pulled ahead, yelling in glee. But the engine picked up speed. Puffing out clouds of smoke, it roared past the galloping ponies. The engineer blew a loud blast on his whistle.

Frightened out of their wits, the braves veered away. They all slipped over the sides of their ponies away from the monster, clinging fast with an arm and a leg as they did in battle. Spotted Tail clapped a hand over his mouth, the Indian way of showing amazement.

By the time the ride ended it was noon. The Sioux were invited to have dinner with the workmen. Everyone ate sitting on the ground in the open. The cooks served big tin plates heaped up with boiled beef, potatoes, beans, bread and pie. But at first the braves would not eat a bite. They thought the food might be poisoned. When they saw the white men eating, though, they fell to and ate greedily.

Now they were ready to leave. And suddenly Spotted Tail was through acting friendly. With a fierce scowl he declared that he and his warriors wanted all they could carry away of the good food, the guns and the bullets. If the white men did not give them what they wanted, he said, he would come back with many more warriors and take everything.

The brave who spoke English told this to Captain Clayton, who was the track boss. Angrily Clayton shouted back:

"All right. Now you tell him what I say."

Then, shaking his fist under Spotted Tail's nose, he dared him to come back, with as many warriors as he could muster.

Without a word the chief sprang on his pony and galloped off. His braves followed. "That was the last we ever saw of them. They had seen the guns," young Mr. Lockwood wrote in his diary.

So it was that the Sioux first learned about the "fire road." The name of the railroad was the Union Pacific. One day it would form part of a rail line stretching two thousand miles from the Missouri River to the Pacific Ocean. The men who were building it were bringing a whole new way of life to the Great Plains.

Perhaps in a dim way, Spotted Tail and his braves realized this.

2. General Jack and Brother Dan

Men first began to talk about a railroad across America early in the 1800's. But many people thought it would never be built. The western country was too vast and wild, they said. They were afraid that such a railroad would cost too much money.

In those days, folk who went west across the Great Plains rode in wagons pulled by oxen or mules. They used ancient trails made by the buffaloes and the Indians. In time these came to be called the Oregon Trail, the California

Trail, and others. The travelers had to wade across rivers. They climbed through high mountain passes and plodded over barren deserts.

Sometimes they got lost. Some were caught in icy blizzards, or starved, or were killed by hostile Indians.

Even when none of these things happened, the trip took many months. Travelers who were in a hurry could ride on the Overland Stage line. But even by stagecoach it took at least two weeks to go from Missouri to San Francisco. And the passengers were bruised and jolted as the coaches bumped along the rough roads.

Travelers on the Oregon Trail stop for the night on the lonely prairie in this drawing by W. M. Cary.

People who settled on the Pacific Coast felt lonely and far from their friends. Businessmen needed a faster, cheaper way to bring goods and products from the east. The men who ran the government in Washington began to see that a railroad was needed to hold the United States together and to make it grow.

At last Congress passed a law granting loans of money and giving free government land to encourage the railroad builders. Two companies were formed. One started to build eastward from Sacramento, California. The other was the Union Pacific which started to build west from Omaha, Nebraska.

A grading crew, using only pickaxes and shovels, digs a roadbed for the mighty Union Pacific.

This early model steam shovel blasts a cut through a stretch of hilly land.

First, surveyors were sent out across the plains and mountains to map a route for the railroad. Grading crews followed them. Blasting rocks and digging through the hills, they worked to make an even roadbed for the rails. Then the track-layers came along.

Two brothers named Casement were given a contract to lay the Union Pacific track. They were small men. General Jack Casement was only five feet, four inches tall. He had won his rank of general, fighting in the Union Army during the War Between the States. His brother Dan was even shorter.

17

But they both were sturdy and strong. A man who knew them once wrote to a friend that "they are a pair of the biggest little men you ever saw."

The first thing the brothers did was to hire a crew of hardy workmen. They paid them three dollars a day, good wages in those days. Then they built the work train that had amazed Spotted Tail and his warriors.

No one had ever thought of a train like that before. But the Casement brothers wanted a

Tender and Engine

Butcher   Flat Car

Mess Hall

rolling headquarters that would always be right on the spot where the work was being done.

Not many people lived in the West in the 1860's. There were no factories. So everything the railroad men needed had to be brought from cities far away in the eastern part of the United States. Most of the supplies were carried by other railroads to St. Louis or St. Joseph, in Missouri. There they were loaded on steamboats with big side wheels, that went splashing up the Missouri River to Omaha.

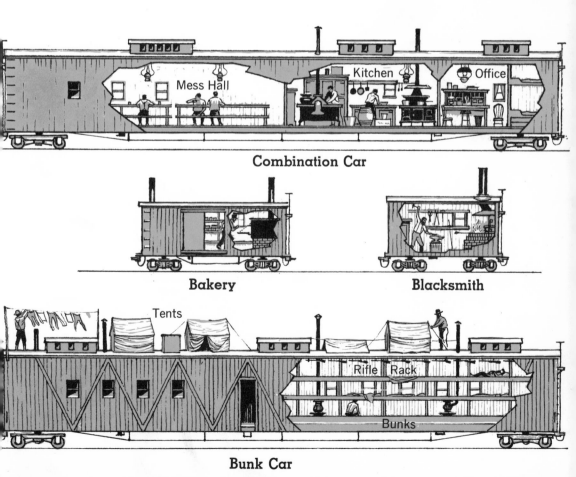

Combination Car

Bakery

Blacksmith

Bunk Car

This shiny locomotive, the first to be used on the
Union Pacific, was brought to Omaha by steamboat.

Even the big locomotives were sent from the
East in this way, piece by piece. At Omaha,
mechanics bolted the parts together. Then the
engines went to work hauling trains of supplies
across the plains to the end of the track.

These trains were called iron trains because
they carried the iron rails used in the track.
Today, of course, railroads run on steel rails.
But at that time there were not enough steel
mills in the whole country to make the tons
and tons of rails that would be needed.

The trains carried many things besides rails,
however. Wooden ties, spikes, tools, food for
the track-layers and the grading crews farther
ahead—all these had to be brought along too.

20

It was Dan Casement's job to see that the iron trains kept running.

General Jack Casement was in charge of the workmen. He was a born leader. And he looked like one, in spite of his small size. He had bright-blue eyes and a bristling red beard. He usually rode a big black horse. When he galloped along the grade cracking his long whip, the men all buckled down and worked hard.

They admired General Jack. He was gruff, and he drove them hard. But he was fair. He never expected a man to work harder than he himself worked.

When the Casement brothers agreed to work for the Union Pacific they promised they would lay a mile of track every day. Hardly anyone believed they could do it. Railroad track never had been laid so fast before.

But Jack and Dan Casement knew their business. And they had some new ideas to try out.

3. A Mile a Day

"Roll out! Rise and shine! Roll out, there!"
The foreman's voice rang loudly through the
bunk car. He hurried down the aisle pounding
on the sides of the bunks, roughly awakening
the men. They yawned and blinked in the dim
lantern light. But they rolled out. There was
a big day's work ahead.

Grumbling as they bumped into each other
in the crowded aisle, the men pulled on shirts,
trousers, and shoes. When they stumbled out-
side, it was still dark. All around the work

train, other men were getting dressed too, for there was not enough room in the bunk cars for everybody. Some men liked to sleep on the ground in the open rather than in the stuffy cars, anyway.

Hardly anyone bothered to wash his face or comb his hair. When Sunday came the men might take a swim in the Platte River, which ran along beside the railroad grade. That would be bathing enough to suit them.

Nearly all of these men had been soldiers in the recent War Between the States. Marching and fighting in all kinds of weather had made them hard and tough. Many were poor, uneducated Irishmen who had come to America because of bad times in their homeland. Others were bold young fellows seeking adventure in the West.

All in all, they were a rough and ready lot.

Breakfast was gobbled in a hurry. Those who could not find room in the mess cars ate in the open. It was much like the meal served to Chief Spotted Tail and his braves. There were beef, beans, potatoes, bread, and hot coffee or tea. And there was plenty. A man could have as many helpings as he wanted.

The sun was just peeping above the horizon

when the men finished eating. Down the track a whistle howled. Here, with its oil fueled headlight shining and its brass bell ringing loudly, came the day's first iron train. Behind the engine were flatcars heaped high with rails. Other flatcars held ties, the wooden timbers on which the rails would be laid. Boxcars were filled with kegs of spikes and other fittings.

Usually, if several iron trains were expected in a day, the workmen put in switches and laid sidetracks. Then the work train was pushed into a sidetrack out of the way. But sometimes the iron trains just pulled in behind the work train on the single track.

Men with sledge hammers knocked away stakes that stuck upright along the flatcars' sides. Rails and ties crashed to the ground, making a great clatter. Quickly, the men opened the boxcars and unloaded them.

Maybe the train had brought some parts for a bridge being built over a stream some distance ahead. These, with the supplies for the grading camps, were stowed in wagons that stood waiting. The drivers shouted and cracked their whips. The mules dug their hooves into the ground. The heavy wagons rolled off in clouds of dust.

Iron gangs begin work as wagons heavily loaded with
supplies start for grading camps.

On the track in front of the train, small
four-wheeled cars, called lorries, were loaded
with rails, ties, and all the other things used
in the track. The first lorry car was pushed
forward. Waiting men seized the ties and laid
them in place on the grade. Then the iron
gangs stepped up.

Four of the best men in the crew made up
an iron gang. A gang worked on each side of
the track. At a command from the foreman,
the first man in each gang took hold of a rail
and pulled it out over a roller in the front of
the lorry car.

As it came clear, the others stepped up and

took hold of the rail, too. The huge rails were
28 feet long. And they weighed more than 200
pounds apiece.

"Down!" shouted the foreman.

The gangs dropped the rails on the ties.
They fitted their ends into iron clamps, called
chairs. They gauged them, making sure they
were exactly far enough apart to fit the wheels
of engines and cars. As they stepped back the
lorry car was pushed ahead. Out came two
more rails. The whole thing was done over,
again and again.

The iron gangs worked fast. A newspaper man from Chicago once came to watch them. He wrote that "the car rolls forward over the new rails ere their clang in falling has ceased to reverberate."

Now came other men, putting spikes in place along the new rails. Brawny fellows with big sledge hammers, called spike mauls, stepped up. Bang! Bang! Bang! The rails were nailed tightly to the ties underneath. Any man who took more than three blows to drive his spike was scorned as a weakling.

Last of all, men dumped broken rock on the new track and packed it down around the ties. The rock was called ballast. It helped to make the track firm.

The moment a lorry car was empty, the iron gangs tipped it off the track. A loaded one rolled up. The work never stopped. As the track stretched farther and farther ahead, a horse was hitched to each loaded lorry. A small boy on the horse's back yelled and thumped his heels into its ribs. Off it went, flying out to the end of the track at a gallop.

We don't know anything about these boys. Maybe some of them had run away from home

to see the world. Maybe some were the sons
of workmen. Whoever they were, they helped
to build the railroad too.

Sometimes the grade went around curves.
Then the rails had to be bent so they would fit.

A rail was first laid on its side with each end
on a tie. Next, several men stood on it. This
bent a curve into the springy iron. Then, at
one end, a man lifted a sledge hammer high
over his head. The first man standing on the
rail stepped off. Down came the hammer. The
first man stepped back on the rail. The next
man stepped off. And down crashed the sledge
hammer again.

In this way the hammer man worked his way along the rail's whole length. When he had finished, there was the curve, as pretty as you please.

A telegraph line was part of the railroad, too. So a telegraph crew worked right along beside the track-layers. They dug holes in the ground. Then poles were unloaded from wagons and placed upright in the holes. Another wagon carried big spools of wire. Men unrolled the wire and strung it along the poles.

Nobody stopped to rest until noon, when the

Workers perch on top of newly erected telegraph poles stringing wire to carry messages along the track.

Work crews in Utah stop for a noonday meal along a wooded bit of track.

workmen had an hour off for dinner. Then back to work they went. They didn't stop again until the sun sank and it grew dark.

At last the foreman cried, "Lay off!"

Through the soft prairie dusk, locomotives pushed the work train slowly out to the end of the new track. Lamplight gleamed from the kitchen and mess cars. The cooks had a hot supper all ready.

Tired though they were, the men laughed and joked as they filled their plates. They were pleased because they had done a good day's work. These men took a fierce pride in being good track-layers. They were like a well-drilled army.

Before long they were doing much better than the mile a day the Casement brothers had promised. They laid two miles of track a day; three miles; five miles. They once laid more than eight miles in a single day. Nothing could stop them.

It was hard, back-breaking work and Sunday was their only day of rest. But they didn't mind. They had some good times, too, as the Union Pacific kept moving west.

This railroad crew poses in front of a Casement construction train.

4. High Times on the Prairie

It was a fine, crisp October day. A locomotive steamed slowly down the track near Kearney, Nebraska. No cars were coupled on behind, but men with rifles sat on the pilot, or cow-catcher, in front. Other men were perched on top of the stack of wood that was piled in the tender.

They all seemed in a jolly mood as they gazed eagerly over the prairie. Suddenly, one of them gave a shout. Beside the track in the distance stood a big, shaggy buffalo.

City gentlemen hunt buffaloes at a safe distance from
the rampaging animals.

A story in an old newspaper, the Omaha
Weekly Herald, tells us what happened next:
"Spencer Smith, the engineer, put on steam
to head the giant off. We succeeded and
got within a hundred yards and he crosses
the track. He proves to be an immense bull
and as he speeds along, about forty shots
are fired at him. Mr. Kinsley, the best shot
in the party, has evidently struck him, as
he pauses . . . He halts and turns around,
when several other well-directed shots from
the same unerring hand bring him to the
ground."

That particular buffalo hunt was put on for a party of newspaper editors who went out west to see the new railroad. Buffaloes were often hunted that way along the Union Pacific.

It was one of the signs of changing times and new ways coming.

For many years people in the eastern states had read and heard tales of the wild land beyond the Missouri River. Now they wanted to see the famous railroad that was being built across that land. Many visitors like that party of editors came flocking west.

The men who ran the Union Pacific were glad, for they wanted people to know about their railroad company, and to buy stock in it. So they always did their best to show their visitors a good time.

The workmen were glad too. Buffalo hunts were only part of the fun they had when guests came on excursions to the end of the track.

The greatest excursion of all took place in the fall of 1866.

Noted senators and congressmen were invited. So were generals of the army, and important businessmen and bankers. A few noblemen even came all the way from Europe. Many of the men brought their wives.

The party gathered at Omaha. A special train was waiting there, made up of nine of the finest passenger cars the railroad owned. To pull the cars, there were two engines, polished till they glittered, and draped with big American flags.

As the train rolled down the track, two brass bands marched through the cars playing lively tunes. One of the best restaurant men from Chicago had been hired, with all his cooks and waiters, to fix and serve the meals.

When evening came the train stopped. A camp had been pitched beside the track, with a comfortable tent for every guest. Dinner was cooked over great, open fires. There were such things to eat as roasted antelope and bear meat, wild turkey and rabbit potpie.

After dinner a band of Pawnee Indians appeared at the camp.

Unlike the Sioux, the Pawnees were friendly to the "fire road." In fact, some of their best braves worked for the U.S. Army as scouts. Now these scouts had come to do a war dance for the visitors. But when they began to prance about in the flickering firelight, screaming their shrill war cries, many of the guests became frightened.

The army officers who had come along had a hard time assuring the ladies in the party that they were not going to be scalped. The railroad men thought this was a great joke.

At dawn the next morning everybody was awakened by another chorus of warwhoops. But it was only the Pawnees again. After breakfast they put on a sham battle against other Pawnees who pretended to be Sioux.

The guests watched, open-mouthed, as ponies dashed back and forth through clouds of dust. Screaming braves waved tomahawks and shot arrows. At last the make-believe Sioux were beaten. They galloped off, while the guests clapped and cheered.

The train went on. Once it stopped so that the gentlemen could go swimming in the Platte River. Of course, there was a buffalo hunt along the way.

At the end of the track, Casement brothers' iron gangs were all ready to show the visitors how they laid the rails. You may be sure they were at their best, too, and worked as they never had worked before.

Union Pacific Railroad Museum Collection

Members of the excursion pose under a sign near the end of the finished track as some Pawnees look on.

That night, after another hearty dinner in the open air, the guests were treated to a band concert. Then, just as they were wondering what would happen next, there was a bang and a flash of light. A skyrocket shot into the air. It was the signal for a fireworks show to begin. More skyrockets and Roman candles burst in sprays of vivid color. Big firecrackers boomed. Pinwheels fizzed and sputtered.

The show lasted for an hour. When the guests went to bed in their tents, their heads were whirling from all the wonderful sights they had seen.

In the morning the train headed back to Omaha.

The guests were so pleased with their trip that many of them bought stock in the Union Pacific Company when they got home. Of course, this was just what the officials of the railroad had hoped they would do.

As for the railroad workers, they got busy at their jobs again. The track still had a long, long way to go. There were all sorts of hardships ahead. There was danger, too.

Many hostile Indians, like Spotted Tail and his warriors, still hated the railroad.

5. A Wreck at Plum Creek

Chief Spotted Tail had found the Casement brothers' crew too strong to attack. But that didn't keep other Indians from raiding smaller groups of railroad men all along the Union Pacific line.

The U.S. Army sent soldiers to guard the railroad. The workers themselves always carried guns, too. And they were good fighters. But the Indians often caught them by surprise. They would dash suddenly over the flat plains

42

on their swift ponies and strike like lightning.

They killed and scalped their victims and rode off before the soldiers could catch them. Again and again this happened.

No one knew when or where they might strike next.

On the night of August 6, 1867, six railroad workmen set out on a handcar from the small station called Plum Creek. This was a little four-wheeled car with handlebars which had to be pumped up and down to make it go. The railroad telegraph line was out of order, and the workmen were looking for the place where the wire was broken, so they could fix it.

Railroad workers always carried rifles with them for protection against attacking Indians.

They had gone only a few miles when dark shapes suddenly loomed up beside the track. War cries rang out. The next moment the handcar hit something and went flying off the track. The men tumbled every which way.

A band of Indians had pulled a tie from under the rails and fastened it across the track.

In an instant the men were struck down. Only the foreman of the crew, William Thompson, managed to jump up and run. But a warrior on horseback overtook him and knocked him flat with a blow of his rifle butt. Leaping to the ground, the warrior drew his knife and scalped him.

44

Gritting his teeth, poor Thompson had to lie still and pretend he was dead. It was his only chance.

But as the brave leaped back on his pony he dropped the scalp. Dazed and hurt though he was, Thompson crawled over and got it. He struggled to his feet and staggered down the track, still clutching the bloody scalp. He thought it might be sewed back on his head if he should be lucky enough to get away alive.

In the meantime, the Indians were dragging more ties out from under the track. They broke two of the rails and piled the ties in the gap. Then they sat down to wait.

Indians tear up the ties and rails of a hated "fire road" so they can capture the next train.

A courageous engineer and his crew were not able to
outrun a band of attacking Indians.

After a while they saw a headlight. A freight train was coming. Jumping on their ponies again, they dashed to meet it.

When he saw them in his headlight beam the engineer of the train put on speed. He was sure he could outrun the ponies. Too late, he saw the pile of ties ahead. With a terrible crash the engine hit them. It plunged off the rails and turned over.

The engineer was flung out of his cab window, badly hurt. The Indians pounced on him and killed him without mercy. The fireman was crushed against the hot boiler of the engine and burned to death. The cars in the train smashed up against the engine and tender. Burning wood spilled out of the locomotive firebox and set all of the wooden cars on fire.

Soon the flames were roaring high.

The train's conductor and three other men jumped off the caboose at the rear end. They knew there was another train coming. Running back down the track and waving their lanterns, they managed to stop it just in time. They climbed aboard. At once the engineer began to back up. He didn't stop till they reached Plum Creek.

But the Indians were far too busy to chase them just then.

The wrecked train was full of all kinds of goods meant for towns and army posts farther west. From the burning boxcars the braves pulled shiny new rifles, rolls of cloth, clothing, things to eat. There was a barrel of whiskey, too.

Never had those Indians been so rich before!

All night long the braves drank and sang and danced. The telegraph operator at Plum Creek tried to get help from Omaha, but it was no use. When the army finally sent a troop of soldiers, the Indians had gone.

Then at last the railroad men could clear away the wreckage and mend the track. Once again the trains started to run.

Poor William Thompson took his scalp back to Omaha. A doctor there tried to sew it back on his head, but the operation was a failure.

Thompson was an Englishman. He went back home soon afterward. He had had his fill of working on the railroad in the wild West, and no wonder.

Most of the workers stuck to their jobs, though. It took more than Indians to scare them. More men were hired as the rails ran

westward. More and more people followed the work crews. Some of them opened stores to sell things to the men who were building the railroad.

Towns sprang up along the grade. Some were far out in front of the track-layers. People hurried to get the best locations. Then they waited impatiently for the rails to come.

One of the biggest of these railroad towns was Cheyenne.

Bear River City, 965 miles west of Omaha, was one of the towns hastily built along the railroad route.

6. The Magic City

General Jack Casement and his iron gangs arrived at Cheyenne on November 13, 1867. They had brought the end of the track more than 500 miles from Omaha.

The very next evening the first passenger train pulled in. Almost 4,000 people were waiting by the new Union Pacific depot. The town already had a brass band. It probably wasn't a very good band, but it played loudly as the engine chugged up and stopped.

Along Eddy Street, the main street, torches and kerosene lamps burned brightly. Gaudy signs hung everywhere. THE MAGIC CITY GREETS THE CONTINENTAL RAILWAY, read one. Another greeted General Jack with OLD CASEMENT, WE WELCOME YOU!

The people of Cheyenne were proud of their town. They called it "The Magic City of the Plains," because it had sprung up like magic.

But the travelers who got off that first train must have wondered what to think of it, for it wasn't a pretty place at all.

It was built along both banks of a little stream named Crow Creek. The streets were

dusty and full of ruts. To north, south, and east lay the flat desolate gray plains. Westward, the land rose toward a tall mountain range thirty miles away. This was a spur of the Rockies known then as the Black Hills.

The Great Plains ended here, and now the railroad would have to go up through the mountains. That would be hard going. It would take even more workmen and supplies than before. Extra engines would be needed to pull trains up the steep slopes.

The U. S. Army had built Fort Russell nearby, to guard the railroad from the Indians. So it was a good place for a town to grow.

Two big hotels were being built with lumber that had been brought by wagon all the way from Denver. But most of the other buildings were small and crude. Many of the builders had run out of planks and boards, and used scraps of canvas instead. Many storekeepers were doing business in tents. The things they sold were just stacked inside, or hung from poles overhead to save space.

Most of the people lived in tents, too. Some who couldn't find anything better had dug caves in the banks of Crow Creek. They hung blankets or buffalo hides over the fronts to keep out the cold.

Everything looked so poor and flimsy that one traveler wrote to his family at home saying that Cheyenne was "a standing insult to all the winds that blow."

Yet Cheyenne was growing fast. Even as the crowd was welcoming that first passenger train on November 14, a long freight train pulled in too. On its flatcars were piled more tents, lumber from old buildings, furniture, and goods of all kinds.

A trainman jumped off, waved his hat to the crowd and yelled:

"Gentlemen, here's Julesburg."

Cheyenne, Wyoming as it appeared in 1868, one year
after the arrival of the Union Pacific Railroad.

Julesburg had been another town some miles
east. The people there had simply torn everything down, loaded it on the cars and moved
on to Cheyenne. Nothing was left of Julesburg
but a dump heap.

Everyone wanted to get some of the money
which the railroad men had to spend.

The track-layers stayed in town for two
weeks. They were busy putting in switches and
laying many sidetracks for the iron trains.
They built big warehouses to hold all the new
supplies that would be coming on from Omaha.
Then the work train pulled out again.

General Jack was anxious to get over the Black Hills before the winter's snows began.

He didn't quite make it, however. The first blizzard came when the end of the track still was ten miles from the summit. The ground froze hard as rock. So he pulled the work train back to Cheyenne and laid off his workmen for the winter.

All those railroad men crowded the town still more. They were hard, rough men, all the more so since they had nothing to do. And still more people kept coming to Cheyenne.

They were all sorts of people, from all over the country.

It was hard to dig a locomotive out of the huge snow drifts after a blizzard on the Wyoming plains.

7. All Sorts of People

The boys who rode the lorry-car horses for the track-layers must have thought Cheyenne was an exciting place. We can imagine some of the things such a boy saw as he walked along Eddy Street.

Perhaps he had to jump out of the way of a Wells Fargo and Company Overland Stage coach hurrying out of town. Mud and snow splashed from the hooves of its six prancing horses. High on the seat the driver shouted and tugged on the reins. Beside him sat a guard with a rifle across his knees.

Through the coach windows the boy might see the passengers inside. Some of them would be dressed in fine clothes, with fur-collared coats and stylish felt or derby hats. They were probably salesmen or businessmen.

Some would be bearded and shaggy, dressed in mackinaw coats and heavy boots. Maybe they were miners or ranchers or lumbermen.

These people might be going to California or Nevada or Denver, or to the new gold mines far up in Montana Territory. Almost everybody traveling west rode on the Union Pacific trains to Cheyenne first. Then they went on from there.

A thousand freight wagons with canvas tops waited at Cheyenne for the start of the spring hauls westward. The burly men who drove them were called bullwhackers or muleskinners. The streets were full of them, swaggering about with their long whips of braided rawhide.

They were experts with these whips. They liked to show off by whirling them around their heads and making them crack like gunshots.

Looking about him, the boy might see the blue uniforms of soldiers from Fort Russell. He would surely see plenty of railroad men,

too, in soot-stained caps and rough work clothes. Many had big red or blue handkerchiefs, called bandannas, tied about their necks.

But when they were off duty, many railroad men dressed in the finest clothes. With their big gold or silver watches and thick watch chains, they looked like rich men. It was hard to tell what kind of work a man did just by looking at him.

There might be buffalo hunters just in off the plains, still dressed in dirty, greasy buckskin garments. Big piles of hides from the

Hunters stretch and press buffalo hides close by the railroad tracks that will carry them East.

buffaloes they had killed were usually stacked beside the railroad tracks, waiting to be shipped east and tanned into leather.

Fierce fights often broke out among all these different men. Sometimes they fought with their fists. But many carried guns, too. On some days the Cheyenne newspaper, *The Daily Leader*, printed a whole column with the heading, LAST NIGHT'S SHOOTINGS.

After the railroad came, some of the newer buildings along Eddy Street looked quite fine. These had been built in whole sections at the lumberyards far off in Chicago. Then the sections were shipped out to Cheyenne on railroad flatcars. Carpenters there just stood the sections up and nailed them together.

The wood in some of these buildings was painted to look like brick or stone. But they were frail and poorly made, just the same.

The town's many theaters and "dancing saloons" ran all day and all night too. The lively music of fiddles, accordions, and pianos could be heard along Eddy Street. Most of these places were just huge tents with plank dance floors. On one side stood a long bar where whiskey was sold. On the other stood rows of gambling tables.

The audience of an early Cheyenne theater included rough workmen and railroad travelers.

Hundreds of men crowded around the tables, playing cards or dice or other games. Most of them were soon cheated out of their money, for Cheyenne was full of thieves and swindlers. Many a man was robbed and murdered just for the few dollars in his pocket. But the criminals were hardly ever punished. There was very little law in Cheyenne that winter.

There were good, respectable people too, however. Many of the railroad workers and other men brought their wives and families. Living in cold, drafty huts or tents, they must have had a hard time. The food they ate was rough and plain, like the food the Casement iron gangs had. It probably wasn't as good, though, nor as plentiful.

We don't really know much about these people, for they minded their own business and did little that would attract attention.

But an old copy of *The Daily Leader* tells us that the town's first school was opened on a cold January day in 1868. It was just a log building with one room. We don't know who the teacher was. But 200 boys and girls went to that school.

A few weeks later, a minister named J. W. Cook came to town and held church services.

Grading crews and wagons move into the mountains.

Then came spring. On the first day of April, 1868, the grading crews moved out of town with 1,000 wagonloads of tools, equipment, and supplies. A Casement brothers' work train chugged out toward the mountains once more.

Many of the storekeepers followed, to start new towns farther along the line. Most of the thieves and gamblers moved on to those new towns.

All of a sudden Cheyenne became a much smaller, quieter place. It didn't die, though. The railroad was still there, with jobs for many people.

8. Working on the Railroad

Most boys in old Cheyenne hoped to work on the railroad when they grew up. And many of them did. It was a hard, dangerous life. But it was exciting too.

A boy might start as a call boy. It was his job to tell the engineers, firemen, and brakemen when the time came for them to go out on their trains.

Sometimes all he had to do was go to their homes or boardinghouses and wake them up. But if they were not there he had to go hunting for them all over town. It might be a cold, stormy midnight. Maybe it was raining. That made no difference.

The call boy worked for twelve hours at a stretch, either day or night. This was called a "trick." Often he was kept running during his whole trick.

But he liked the job because he learned to know the men who ran the trains. They told him stories of fast runs they had made, of wrecks and narrow escapes. He learned what it really was like to be a railroader.

When he was not busy calling train crews, the call boy helped with odd jobs at the round-house. In this way he learned more about the railroad.

The engineer manages to stop just in time to avoid a crash with an approaching train.

The roundhouse was a kind of big barn where the engines were kept. It was called that because it really was round. If you could look down upon one from up above, it would look very much like a big capital letter C.

There were tracks in the roundhouse like the spokes in a great wheel. And at the open space in the center of the C was a turntable. This was a short track made so that it could be turned around in a circle. It was used to turn the engines when the men ran them in or out of the roundhouse.

Cheyenne's roundhouse was built of bricks. It was one of the biggest, sturdiest buildings in town. Smoke from the engines had turned its walls black and sooty. A dense cloud of smoke usually hung in the air above it.

Inside, the roundhouse was a dirty, noisy, confusing place. Locomotives grumbled and roared. Steam hissed in their boilers. There was always a mighty clatter as mechanics and boilermakers worked at repairing the engines. The air was filled with the smell of smoke, steam, oil, and hot metal.

It was a smell no old-time railroad man ever forgot. Some of them used to say they had valve oil in their blood.

After he had been working as call boy for a while, a bright young fellow might then get a chance to "go firing." Or he might even become a brakeman.

Keeping his engine looking spick-and-span was part of a fireman's duties. He polished the bell and the long, shiny boiler. He swept the cab floor and filled the big headlight with oil. He made sure there was plenty of wood and water in the tender. Then he built a hot fire in the firebox under the boiler.

While he did all this, the engineer took a

big copper oil can with a long spout and carefully oiled all the engine's moving parts.

At last they chugged out onto the main track. The engine was coupled to its train. Off they went.

Now the fireman was kept busy throwing big chunks of wood into the blazing firebox. That kept the water in the boiler turning to steam to make the engine run. It took a lot of steam. The fireman didn't get a chance to sit down very much, you may be sure. But he didn't mind. A good fireman would become an engineer some day.

The engineer sat on the right side of the cab. He moved a long lever, called a throttle, to run the engine faster or more slowly. He kept a sharp eye on the track ahead, and watched for the signals that stood by the track.

When he had to stop his train, the engineer blew "down brakes" on the whistle. That was a special signal. It told the brakeman of the train to get busy and turn big iron wheels that set the brakes on each car.

On a passenger coach this wasn't hard to do. But in those early days most Union Pacific passenger trains were "mixed." That is, they had freight cars too. And a brakeman had to climb up and run over the tops of these to get to the brake wheels. He had to jump from one swaying, jolting car to the next one, sometimes for the train's whole length.

If he tripped or lost his balance he might easily fall under the wheels of the train or be crushed between the cars. And that would be the end of him.

But, like the fireman, a brakeman had something to work for. Some day he would become a conductor.

The conductor was the boss of the whole train. He was like the captain of a ship. In those days on the Union Pacific, he didn't often wear a fine uniform with a blue coat and brass buttons. Usually, he was dressed in rough work clothes like the rest of the train crew. But even the engineer had to take orders from him.

The conductor took tickets and watched out for the passengers. He kept a record of every freight car in the train, showing what was in it and where it was going. His most important duty, though, was making sure the train orders were obeyed.

Train orders were messages sent over the telegraph line beside the track. They told the conductor just where his train should go into

A well-dressed conductor takes tickets from the passengers on a train traveling west.

The members of a train crew enjoy a friendly chat in the caboose.

a sidetrack so that the trains going in the other direction could pass. If this wasn't done the two trains might crash head-on on the single track.

So the conductor had to keep his wits about him every minute. He had to see that everybody else in the train crew did too.

There were all sorts of things that might go wrong. The old iron rails were not very strong. Sometimes they broke, causing wrecks. Rainstorms might wash the earth and ballast out from under the track, so the trains couldn't pass. In winter, snow often blocked the rails. A train might be stalled for hours, or even days.

Once in a while a great herd of buffaloes would get in the way. That caused still more delays. And for a long time, hostile Indians went on raiding the "fire road," too.

When the call boy came knocking at a railroad man's door, his wife and family never knew when he would be home again. As they said good-bye they always hugged him tightly and added in a low voice, "Be careful."

The crew of this stalled train tries to frighten the buffalo off the tracks with a spray of steam.

The crew of a Union Pacific train shoots it out with hostile Indians.

Of course there were many, many other jobs on the railroad besides running the trains. All kinds of repairmen were needed to work on engines and cars. There were men who worked the switches when cars were moved from one track to another. The men who did this job were called switchmen.

Every station along the line had a telegraph operator. He was often known as a "brass pounder," on account of the brass telegraph key he used. The key was clicked up and down to make sounds, called dots and dashes, which stood for different letters of the alphabet.

Train orders and other messages were spelled out by means of these dots and dashes.

Some workmen spent all their time going up and down the railroad track. Sometimes they rode handcars and sometimes they walked. They looked for broken or worn places in the track and fixed them.

Other men, called clerks, were busy all day just keeping straight all the written records it took to run the railroad. In fact, a list of all

Storage tanks along the track contain needed water for the locomotive.

the different kinds of jobs on a railroad would take up a whole book by itself. Thousands of men were needed to fill these jobs.

This was true even though the railroad was not yet finished. Far ahead, the Union Pacific graders and track-layers still worked on. They crossed mountains and deserts. From the west the graders and track-layers of the other company, the Central Pacific, were working hard to meet them.

The year 1868 passed. Still the men of the two companies worked on and on. They were getting closer together with every day and week that passed.

Soon people could see that the end of the job was in sight.

The Union Pacific and the Central Pacific Railroads
were joined at Promontory Summit on May 10, 1869.

9. The Grand Tour

It was past noon on Monday, May 10, 1869. A crowd of people stood around the Union Pacific Railroad depot at Cheyenne. They waited impatiently in the hot sun.

Groups of men and women talked soberly together. Some of the men kept taking their watches out of their pockets and looking at them. Boys and girls ran about, laughing and playing. They should have been in school, but on this day everyone was too excited to worry about a thing like that.

Inside the depot, the leading men of the town were standing around a table with a shiny telegraph key on it. The telegraph operator sat there, waiting.

Suddenly, the key began to click. It was a very short message: just one word. The operator, the only man there who could understand it, jumped up with a glad shout:

"Done!"

Five hundred miles away at a place called Promontory Summit, in Utah, the tracks of the Union Pacific and the Central Pacific had met. The head men of the two companies had driven

a golden spike into the last tie to join the rails together. The railroad to the Pacific Ocean was finished.

In an instant that one word, "Done!" flashed along the telegraph wires all over America. Everywhere the people began to celebrate. In most of the big cities they marched in parades and listened to patriotic speeches. In many places they danced and sang in the streets. Cannons were fired. Church bells rang.

We don't know exactly what the people did in Cheyenne. *The Daily Leader* tells us only that all the gunpowder in town was fired off, so it must have been a noisy time.

To tell the truth, the people probably didn't stop to think of all the reasons why this was a great day for Cheyenne, and for America.

Soon, though, they could see new things happening.

It seemed that everyone was eager to ride on the new railroad. It was the longest one in the whole world at that time. Travelers came from all over the world to take the "Grand

Many people crowd this railroad station awaiting the arrival of the Union Pacific.

Tour" from the Atlantic to the Pacific, as it was called. Never before had there been a trip like that.

From New York City the travelers rode on other railroads to Chicago. There they changed to a second railroad that took them as far as Council Bluffs, Iowa. Then they had to get off and ride on a ferryboat across the Missouri River to Omaha. There at last they got on board the Union Pacific train to California.

They still had a five-day ride before they got to Sacramento. But even the fastest coaches of the old Overland Stage had taken seventeen days.

The railroad's new Pullman Palace cars were the finest that could be built. They had soft seats of red or green plush. At night the seats were unfolded and made into beds, called berths. Curtains and draperies of rich velvet hung at the windows. The walls were of rare, polished woods.

Today, we wouldn't think all this was so grand. The cars were lighted by oil lamps, for there was no electricity in those days. In winter, small stoves burning wood or coal kept the passengers warm. They didn't do a very good job of it, though.

It was a real luxury for passengers to travel in one of the first pullman cars on the Union Pacific.

The cars were fastened together by couplers that were nothing but short pieces of chain. They rattled and jerked as the train chugged along. It was dangerous to go from one car to another, for there were wide gaps in between. Dust and smoke from the engine blew in through the windows.

But the travelers didn't mind.

Sitting in their seats they could look out and see many new and wonderful sights. Sometimes, herds of deer, buffaloes, or antelopes grazed beside the track. Sometimes the train passed prairie dog villages that covered many square miles. Each little prairie dog–a kind of wild rat–would be sitting up straight, like a tent peg on the mound of earth by its hole.

Now and then the conductor would point out old forts that had been built for protection against savage Indians. But by this time all the hostile Indians had been driven far away from the railroad.

Once in a while the train might pass covered wagons and their ox teams plodding along the old Overland Trail. A few people still went west this way. But the days of the Overland Trail were almost ended, now that the railroad had been built.

Trains stopped just long enough for travelers to eat
a hasty lunch at station dining rooms like this one.

When mealtimes came, the train stopped at
some station along the line. All the passengers
got off and went into the station to eat, for
there were no dining cars. But many of the
stations grew famous for their delicious food.
An Englishman wrote this about a breakfast
he ate in a town called Sidney, in Nebraska:

"There were given us eight little dishes
apiece, containing hot beefsteak, two slices
of cold roast antelope, a bit of cold chicken,
ham and poached eggs, a couple of boiled
potatoes, two sticks of sweet corn, stewed
tomatoes and four thin buckwheat 'hot
cakes' laid one on top of the other."

The westbound express passenger train, Number 3, arrived at Cheyenne at 8:45 in the morning, just in time for a breakfast like this. It was one of the big events in Cheyenne's day, and the station was one of the busiest, most important places in town.

We can imagine that the boys and girls often went there on a Saturday or Sunday morning to watch Number 3 pull in. How they must have stared as the passengers got off the cars and hurried into the dining room.

Perhaps they made a little fun of the people they called "dudes from the city." But they were impressed, all the same.

The men wore fine, long coats and tight trousers of broadcloth or corduroy. Their vests, or waistcoats, were bright-colored and they wore tall silk hats or hard round ones of felt.

The ladies looked very pretty in their dresses with long, full skirts and lots of flounces and fancy bows. Around their shoulders were traveling shawls of silk or wool. Their hats had gay feathers and make-believe flowers and they usually wore dark veils over their faces, to keep out the smoke and dust.

As the train stood waiting, the boys and girls could peer through the windows of the

cars. The rooms in their own homes, they thought, were surely not as grand as those railroad cars.

Such sights made the children think of the wide world beyond Cheyenne. Perhaps they dreamed of being well-to-do travelers themselves some day.

They didn't know it, but these splendid trains were just the first sign of the changing times the railroad would bring.

10. Years of Change

Before long the people of Cheyenne began to see a new kind of stranger on the streets of their town. They were as different from the tourists on the Grand Tour as different could be.

They came riding in from the plains on dashing ponies. They wore broad-brimmed hats and high-heeled boots and big leather leggings, called chaps. They had pistols in holsters at their belts, and coils of rope at their saddle bows.

They were cowboys. They too had come to Cheyenne because the railroad was there.

For many years, cattle ranchers from Texas had been driving their herds of steers northward and eastward. At first they just wanted to reach the railroads to ship the steers to market. But soon they saw that the grass on the Great Plains made good feed for the steers. There were few settlers there, and lots of room for their herds.

So some of the cattlemen stayed. Some rich men from England invested their money in the

Boisterous cowboys gallop down the main street of an early western town.

land, too. As time passed, big ranches sprang up all over western Nebraska, Wyoming, and Colorado.

Large pens, or corrals, were built in every town along the railroad track. Cowboys drove the steers in at roundup time. They put them in the corrals and kept them until they could be loaded into cattle cars and sent east.

Cheyenne became one of the biggest cow towns in all the west. Once again it became a wild and lawless place, too. The cowboys were as tough and hard as the graders and

Cattlemen cracking bullwhips drive frightened cattle into the boxcar of a western railroad.

This is a tense moment as outlaws rob a train. In the distance a posse rushes to catch the robbers.

track-layers who built the railroad had been.

But times were changing. The railroad was bringing still other people west. These were poor workmen and farmers. Some of them came from the crowded cities in the eastern states. Many came from countries in Europe, far across the sea. They had been oppressed and treated badly at home. Now they wanted freedom and land of their own.

The railroad wanted them to come, because they bought the land along the track.

These poor folk didn't ride on the fine

Uncomfortable emigrant trains replaced the covered wagons which had previously carried settlers west.

passenger trains like the people who took the Grand Tour, though. For them the railroad ran "emigrant trains." The fare was cheap, but the cars were dirty and uncomfortable. They had hard wooden seats and tiny windows that let in very little light. For beds the travelers had only hard boards which were laid across the seats.

When they reached their destination, they found that the land they had bought was just barren prairie. They had to work hard, plowing the soil and planting crops. In order to build

90

their own homes, they had to struggle and save for many years.

But most of them stayed. They didn't give up in spite of many hardships.

Thus, slowly, prosperous ranches and farms grew up where once only Indians and wild animals had lived.

In the meantime the railroad too was growing and changing. Now, from the main line, other tracks called branch lines began to stretch out in all directions. They reached new towns. Then the people in those towns could use the railroad too.

When the first rails of wrought iron wore out, new steel ones were laid. They were strong enough to hold up bigger, heavier locomotives. So the trains could be made longer and go faster. After a while cars began to be built of steel too, instead of wood.

Today, many people whose great-grandfathers and great-grandmothers once rode on the Grand Tour now drive their own automobiles over broad, smooth highways. Many travelers now fly across the country in just a few hours, in big jet airplanes. But others still like to travel by passenger train.

Huge trucks now carry many of the goods

that once rolled over the rails, too. Yet the
country has grown so big that modern freight
trains are still needed to keep Americans
supplied with all the things they use.

Mighty diesel locomotives whisk these trains
smoothly and swiftly along the track. The hard
and dangerous jobs are all done by machines
run by electricity now.

The puffing steam engines with their clouds
of smoke are gone. If old Chief Spotted Tail
could come back today he would never know
the "fire road" he fought in the days when
the rails ran west.

Glossary

ballast: broken rock or gravel packed around railroad ties to make a firm bed for the tracks

brass pounder: the name given to a telegraph operator

bullwhacker: the man who drove a covered wagon pulled by oxen

call boy: a boy whose job was to call the train crew to work

chairs: iron clamps which held rails in place on the ties

coupler: a device used to join railroad cars

down brakes: a special signal to a brakeman telling him to put on the train's brakes

fire road: the name Indians gave to the railroad

grade: to make hilly land level or to slope it gradually

handcar: a little four-wheeled railroad car which is moved by pumping its handlebars

iron gang: a group of four men who placed the rails on ties

iron train: a special train used to deliver iron rails and other supplies to the work site

lorry car: a small railroad car drawn by horses which delivered supplies to the track-layers

mackinaw: a heavy woolen cloth often used to make short coats

mess hall: a dining room

muleskinner: the man who drove a covered wagon pulled by mules

pilot: a frame on the front of a locomotive designed to throw obstacles off the track, often called a cowcatcher

roundhouse: a building, equipped with a turntable, used to store and repair locomotives

sidetrack: an extra track next to the main one used to keep a train out of the way of another train

spike maul: a large hammer used to nail rails onto ties

tender: the vehicle attached to a locomotive for carrying fuel and water

ties: wooden beams to which the rails were nailed

train orders: messages sent over the telegraph line to direct the conductor of a train

trick: the period of time worked by a railroad man

turntable: a rotating track on which engines are turned around

work train: a train in which the railroad building crews lived

Index